international classics

international classics

TIME
LIFE
BOOKS

Alexandria, Virginia

Time-Life Books is a division of Time Life Inc.

TIME LIFE INC.
Chairman and CEO   Jim Nelson
President and COO   Steven L. Janas

TIME-LIFE TRADE PUBLISHING
Vice President and Publisher   Neil Levin
Senior Director of Acquisitions and Editorial Resources   Jennifer Pearce
Director of New Product Development   Carolyn Clark
Director of Marketing   Inger Forland
Director of Trade Sales   Dana Hobson
Director of Custom Publishing   John Lalor
Director of Special Markets   Robert Lombardi
Director of Design   Kate L. McConnell

INTERNATIONAL CLASSICS
Project Manager   Jennie Halfant
Technical Specialist   Monika Lynde

This edition first published in the U.K. in 1999 by Hamlyn
Octopus Publishing Group Limited
2–4 Heron Quays
London E14 4JP

Printed in China
10 9 8 7 6 5 4 3 2 1

Library of Congress Cataloging-in-Publication Data
International classics: over 60 simple recipes for elegant home cooking.
   p. cm.
  Includes index.
  ISBN 0-7370-2055-5
   1. Cookery, International.

TX725.A1 I38 2000
641.59--dc21
                                    00-023457

Notes
1 Milk should be whole milk unless otherwise stated.
2 Fresh herbs should be used unless otherwise stated. If unavailable, use dried herbs as an alternative but only half the amount stated.
3 Pepper should be freshly ground black pepper unless otherwise stated; season according to taste.
4 Do not refreeze a dish that has been frozen previously.

contents

6

introduction

Classic recipes are those that are used by generations of cooks, again and again, despite changing fads in food and diet. These are the dishes cooked most often, and for good reason. Originally, these recipes made use of homegrown foods, but now they incorporate exotic ingredients and different cooking styles, as people's horizons have widened over the centuries; these are recipes that have stood the test of time and reflect social history. For example, Kedgeree (a smoked haddock and rice dish) became a popular Anglo-Indian dish during the days of the British Raj, but has stayed popular ever since, even though few people today would recognize its origins. With such wide-ranging influences, classic dishes can be both comforting in their familiarity and exciting in their variety.

Today's classic dishes come from a wide range of other cuisines, and this book brings them together in one volume. The wealth of dishes, some of which have survived for generations, are truly a part of an international culinary heritage. As well as a good choice of favorite recipes from the British Isles, such as Chicken Pot Pie and Lancashire Hot Pots, there are great national dishes from France (Coq au Vin and Cassoulet), Italy (Chunky Minestrone), Spain (Paella), India (Chicken Korma), and South America (Chile con Carne). These dishes have become classics because of their satisfying yet sophisticated simplicity. There are excellent recipes covering all parts of a meal—appetizers, main courses, and desserts—and there are baking recipes and dishes suitable for snacks, light lunches, and late suppers.

Meal Planning
Despite the wide variety of cultures and societies these recipes come from, they can work together surprisingly well, making meal planning from this book a lot of fun. Although there are noticeable differences between the way a chicken dish from France, say, is prepared and one from India—compare the delicate flavorings of a Chicken Véronique with a more heavily spiced but still creamily light Kashmiri Chicken, for instance—they both have in common a good understanding of how to turn a selection of basic ingredients into dishes that both satisfy the appetite and please the senses.

So, there is no need to be afraid of mixing dishes from different regional styles. A fresh Lemon & Avocado Soup can make a fine lead into a substantial main course dish like Carbonnade of Beef or a lighter but more highly spiced dish such as Lamb Tagine. However, an important point to remember when mixing and matching recipes is not to choose dishes so widely different in taste that one will swamp the other.

Getting the Best Out of Ingredients
All the recipes in this book were developed to make the best possible use of locally grown and produced foods—the better the quality of the food, the more tasty and succulent the dishes made from them. Because food today is more mass-produced

"I feel a recipe is only a theme, which an intelligent cook can play each time with a variation."

Madame Benoît

than it was in our parents' or grandparents' time, we have a great many more choices when it comes to selecting and preparing food. Unusual ingredients from all over the world can now be found in our grocery stores and people are increasingly more informed about styles of cooking from other countries as well as the importance of following a healthy diet and food safety.

Care should be taken when buying fresh fish—buy it the day it is to be cooked and look for a plump, firm, shiny, and moist body and a bright, fresh eye that has not sunk into the head. If the fish has too strong and fishy a smell, it is not very fresh. Take care also when selecting smoked haddock—it should always be properly smoked and not dyed a vivid yellow, as this suggests that many additives have been used in its production. Good-quality fish can be bought in most large supermarkets.

Vegetables should always be the freshest possible, with organically grown vegetables having the added bonus of excellent flavor. Always try to prepare vegetables just before they are to be used, as soaking loses valuable vitamins and minerals, and leaving vegetables lying around causes them to lose their fresh crispness. Root vegetables, if young and fresh, may not need peeling, but just a good scrub. For vegetables that do need peeling, use a vegetable peeler, rather than a kitchen knife, to shave off as fine a layer of skin as possible, as most of the vitamins and minerals are found closest to the skin.

Unless they are to be used immediately, it is best not to wash mushrooms. Simply wipe off any of the soil that may be clinging to them with paper towels. Most mushrooms do not need to be peeled.

When choosing stocks and broths at the supermarket, choose canned or frozen stocks, rather than bouillon cubes, which tend to be overly salty and also contain quite high amounts of fat.

Classic Extras

Just as there are many classic recipes, so there are many classic combinations of ingredients, or specially prepared ingredients, used in cooking. Among those that may be used with recipes in this book are:

Beurre manié—equal amounts of all-purpose flour and softened butter are worked together into a paste and stirred into stews and sauces to thicken them.

Bouquet garni—a bunch of fresh herbs tied together and used to flavor soups, stews, and casseroles; it is removed from the cooked dish before serving. A basic bouquet garni combination is sprigs of fresh parsley and thyme and a bay leaf. Fresh marjoram, a piece of celery, and other herbs may be used, too.

Clarified butter—unsalted butter that has been melted and turned into a clear yellow liquid, which can then be heated to a higher temperature than butter during cooking, without burning. To clarify butter, melt the unsalted butter over gentle heat and cook it, without stirring, until it foams. Keep cooking the butter gently until it stops foaming, then set it aside to let the milky solids sink to the bottom of the pan. Strain the liquid through cheesecloth and discard the milky solids.

Vinaigrette—a mixture of oil and vinegar, seasoned with salt and pepper, sometimes flavored with herbs, and used to dress salads or vegetables. The classic mixture is 3 or 4 parts oil to 1 part vinegar, and the classic combination is olive oil and wine vinegar.

Chantilly cream—thick cream whipped to soft peaks and flavored with a little superfine sugar, and 2 or 3 drops of vanilla extract. Serve with hot or cold desserts.

Crumble topping—an all-time favorite hot fruit topping. The basic crumble mixture is 6 parts flour, 3 parts butter, and 2 parts sugar. Mix the flour and sugar together and rub in the butter in small pieces until the mixture resembles breadcrumbs. Spoon the mixture over prepared fresh fruit sprinkled with a little water in a baking dish—apples, apricots, peaches, and rhubarb are top choices. Sprinkle brown sugar over the crumble topping and bake in a preheated oven at 375°F for about 25 minutes.

Fruit fool—another delicious fruit dessert made by whipping thick cream to soft peaks, and lightly mixing it with sweetened puréed fruit. Try for a marbled effect so that the color of the fruit shows in the cream.

Healthy Classic Cooking

Many classic recipes seem less than healthy to today's cooks. Although a certain amount of fat is essential in a healthy diet, much of it can be reduced or eliminated Many recipes use vegetable oil, which has less saturated fat than lard or butter, and cooking methods have also been adapted to cut down on the amount of fat used in the original recipes.

Where once butter and cream were essential, it is now possible to replace them with low-fat dairy products. Yogurt makes a good substitute for cream in creamy sauces, though it is essential not to allow the sauce to boil once the yogurt has been added, or it may curdle. Half-fat crème fraîche makes an excellent and delicious low-fat replacement for cream in desserts.

soups, appetizers & snacks

1 lb. yellow onions, peeled

½ stick (¼ cup) butter

2 tablespoons all-purpose flour

5 cups beef stock

1 tablespoon cognac (optional)

½ teaspoon Dijon mustard

salt and pepper

To Garnish:

6 slices French bread

1 cup grated Swiss cheese

Serves 6
Preparation time: 10 minutes
Cooking time: 40 minutes

1 Slice the onions into fairly thick even rings. Melt the butter in a saucepan. Add the onions and cook over medium heat, stirring constantly, until soft and pale gold in color. Sprinkle in the flour, stir for about 1 minute, then gradually pour in the stock. Bring the mixture to a boil, stirring constantly. Add salt and pepper to taste.

2 Lower the heat and simmer for 20–25 minutes. Add the cognac, if using. Stir in the Dijon mustard. Keep the onion soup hot.

3 Toast the bread for the garnish until it is lightly browned. Sprinkle each slice with grated Swiss cheese. Pour the soup into heatproof bowls and float a slice of cheese-topped toasted bread on each portion. Put the bowls under a preheated broiler until the cheese melts and bubbles. Serve immediately.

■ Traditional French onion soup uses beef stock. For a vegetarian alternative, use vegetable stock. The vegetable stock could be made richer by boiling it for 10 minutes with 1½ cups chopped mushrooms. Strain the stock and use according to the recipe.

french onion soup

chunky minestrone

1 Heat the oil in a large pot. Add the onions, garlic, and diced bacon and cook gently for 5 minutes. Add the chicken stock and bring to a boil. Add the tomatoes and carrots. Cover the pan and cook steadily for 15 minutes, adding a little seasoning, if necessary. At the end of this time, check that there is enough liquid left to cook the cabbage and pasta. If not, add a little more stock or water and bring back to a boil.

2 Add the cabbage, pasta, and peas. Cook for 15 minutes, or until the pasta is tender. Add the canned beans, stir gently, and heat for a few minutes.

3 Serve the soup topped with the grated cheese and herbs.

2 tablespoons olive oil

4 bacon slices, diced

2 onions, finely chopped

2 garlic cloves, finely chopped

2½ cups chicken stock

2 large tomatoes, skinned and chopped

2 carrots, finely grated

1 cup finely shredded green cabbage

2 oz. macaroni

¾ cup frozen peas

1 cup canned vegetarian baked beans with tomato sauce

salt and pepper

Topping:

grated Parmesan cheese

chopped basil and thyme

Serves 4
Preparation time: 15 minutes
Cooking time: 40–45 minutes

lemon & avocado soup

1 Cut the avocados in half and remove the pits and the peel. Either mash the avocado with the lemon zest and juice, or blend it with all the ingredients. Adjust the amount of lemon juice according to taste.

2 If mashing the avocado, gradually add the stock and cream, or yogurt, beating briskly to give a smooth texture.

3 Chill the soup and add the garnish just before serving.

■ To prevent the avocados from turning brown, do not prepare them until you have all of the ingredients at hand. To give a spicier flavor, add a few drops of Tabasco sauce or a pinch of cayenne pepper.

2 medium avocados

1–2 teaspoons finely grated lemon zest

2–3 tablespoons lemon juice

2 cups vegetable or chicken broth

⅔ cup light cream or plain yogurt

salt and pepper

To Garnish:

finely chopped scallions

diced tomato (optional)

Serves 4

Preparation time: 10 minutes

scotch broth

1   Put the lamb, 3 onions, 3 turnips, and 2 carrots into a large pot with the water, salt, and peppercorns. Bring to a boil, cover, and simmer for 3 hours. Let it get quite cold and then remove all the fat. Pour off the stock and set aside. Take the meat off the bones, and discard the fat and the vegetables.

2   Wash out the pan to remove any traces of fat, then return the stock to it, along with all the remaining vegetables and the barley. Cover and simmer for about 40 minutes.

3   Cut the lamb into small pieces, add to the broth, and boil for another 5 minutes until the meat has warmed through. Serve hot.

2 lb. lamb shoulder

5 onions, finely sliced

5 turnips, finely sliced

3 large carrots, finely sliced

2 quarts water

1 teaspoon salt

12 peppercorns

1 leek, finely sliced

2 celery stalks, finely sliced

3 tablespoons barley

Serves 6

Preparation time: 20 minutes plus cooling

Cooking time: 3¾ hours

omelette arnold bennett

1 Mix the smoked haddock with the Parmesan. Season with pepper to taste. Melt the butter in a heavy frying pan or omelette pan and swirl the butter until it completely coats the pan. Do not allow the butter to brown.

2 Pour in the eggs, which should sizzle slightly, then with a spatula, move the eggs into the middle but tip the pan so that the uncooked egg that is left runs over and covers the bottom.

3 When the bottom is just set but the top is still creamy, spoon over the fish and cheese mixture evenly. Pour the cream smoothly on top. Remove the pan from the heat, sprinkle the top with freshly ground pepper, and put under a preheated broiler until it is puffed up and golden.

4 It is not necessary to fold this omelette; simply slide it off the pan, cream side up, onto a hot plate and serve.

10 oz. smoked haddock, cooked, skinned, and flaked

2 tablespoons grated Parmesan cheese

1 teaspoon butter

6 large eggs, lightly beaten

3–4 tablespoons heavy cream

pepper

Serves 2
Preparation time: 15 minutes
Cooking time: 7 minutes

■ This snack or late supper dish was created by a chef at London's Savoy Hotel for the writer Arnold Bennett when he worked in London as a theater critic.

kedgeree

1 Add the rice to boiling, salted water, cover, and simmer on low heat for about 12 minutes, or according to package instructions, until each grain is dry and fluffy, then set aside and keep warm.

2 Poach the haddock in a little water for 10 minutes, drain, and break the fish into large flakes. Meanwhile, hard-boil the eggs, shell them, then cut half an egg into wedges for the garnish; chop the rest.

3 Heat the butter in a large pan and fry the leek for 3 minutes until soft but not colored. Add the fish, cooked rice, and just enough cream to moisten. Heat gently, stirring carefully, so the flakes of fish are not broken. Add the chopped egg to the mixture and season to taste. Spoon the mixture onto warmed serving dishes and garnish with the reserved egg wedges and some finely chopped parsley.

½ cup long-grain rice

1 lb. smoked haddock

2 large eggs

½ stick (¼ cup) butter

1 leek, finely chopped

2–3 tablespoons light cream

salt and pepper

finely chopped parsley, to garnish

Serves 4
Preparation time: 10 minutes
Cooking time: 30 minutes

■ This Anglo-Indian dish originates from the era of the British Raj. It is a very good and filling breakfast or brunch dish. If time is short, cook the rice, eggs, and haddock in advance, and assemble the dish (step 3) just before serving, making sure the ingredients are piping hot.

cornish
pasties

1 To make the pastry, sift the salt and flour into a bowl, then rub in the fat with your fingers until the mixture resembles coarse breadcrumbs. Gradually add enough ice water to make a stiff dough, kneading lightly with your hands until it is smooth. Wrap in plastic wrap and chill for at least 30 minutes. For the filling, mix the meat and vegetables together with the water, and season very well.

2 Roll out the pastry on a floured surface to about ¼ inch thick and cut into 4 circles about 8 inches in diameter. Divide the mixture among the 4 circles, filling only one half of each circle. Dampen the edges with cold water, fold the pastry over to cover the mixture, and press the edges together with a fork or your fingers. Otherwise, put the filling in the middle of the pastry circle and draw up the edges to the center top.

3 Brush the pasties with milk or a little beaten egg and make a small slit on top. Put them on a greased baking sheet and bake in a preheated oven, 425°F, for 15 minutes, then reduce the oven temperature to 350°F, and bake for 35–40 minutes more. Serve the pasties hot or cold.

Pastry:

¼ teaspoon salt

4 cups all-purpose flour

2 sticks (1 cup) butter

6 tablespoons ice water

Filling:

1 lb. finely chopped lean beef or lamb

2 small-to-medium potatoes, coarsely grated

1 small piece of turnip, coarsely grated

3–4 tablespoons cold water

a little milk or egg, to glaze

salt and pepper

Serves 4

Preparation time: 1 hour plus chilling

Cooking time: 50–55 minutes

■ In a traditional Cornish pasty, the meat is finely chopped, not ground, and the vegetables are grated.

irish smoked salmon with scrambled eggs

1 Melt the butter in a saucepan until foaming. Place the eggs in a bowl and mix well with a fork. Add the milk and season to taste.

2 Pour the eggs into the foaming butter. Stir with a wooden spoon over a gentle heat, scraping the bottom of the pan and bringing the outside edges to the middle. The eggs are cooked when they form soft creamy curds and are barely set.

3 Remove from the heat, stir in the cream, if using, the lox, and the chives or dill, and pile onto the hot brown toast on a warmed serving plate. Serve immediately.

1 tablespoon butter

3 large eggs

1 tablespoon milk

1 tablespoon cream (optional)

2 oz. lox (smoked salmon), cut into narrow strips

1 teaspoon finely snipped chives or dill

1–2 slices warm whole-wheat bread, toasted and buttered

salt and pepper

Serves 1	
Preparation time: 5 minutes	
Cooking time: 3–4 minutes	

prosciutto & lemon

1 Arrange the prosciutto on plates with the lemon halves. Season to taste with pepper and serve with buttered whole-wheat toast.

■ Otherwise, serve the prosciutto with melon. Cut 1 sweet, ripe melon into quarters. Drape the slices of ham over them and sprinkle with black pepper.

5–7 oz. prosciutto

1 lemon cut in half, and each half wrapped in a piece of clean cheesecloth (optional)

crushed black peppercorns

buttered whole-wheat toast, to serve

Serves 2

Preparation time: 5 minutes

1 large onion

1 garlic clove

1 lb. pork shoulder

½ cup port

1 teaspoon chopped fresh mint

8 oz. chicken livers, finely chopped

6 slices bacon, finely chopped

1 cup finely chopped mushrooms

1 egg, beaten

salt and pepper

rosemary sprigs, to garnish

Serves 8

Preparation time: 10–15 minutes plus marinating and cooling

Cooking time: 1½ hours

1 Put the onion, garlic, and pork into a food processor and run until smooth. Pour into a bowl, stir in the port and mint, and season to taste. Cover and leave to marinate in the refrigerator overnight.

2 Mix the liver, bacon, and mushrooms into the port mixture. Stir in the egg. Spoon into a foil-lined 1-lb. loaf pan and bake in a preheated oven, 350°F, for 1½ hours. Carefully pour off the fat and leave to cool.

3 To serve, remove the pâté from the pan, place on a serving dish, and garnish with sprigs of rosemary.

pork & port pâté

1 Place the flour in a bowl. Add the butter and rub in with your fingertips until the mixture resembles fine breadcrumbs. Add the egg yolk and enough cold water to mix to a firm dough. Cover and chill for 30 minutes.

2 Roll out the dough on a lightly floured surface and line a 9-inch quiche pan with it. Chill the pastry shell for 30 minutes. Fill with crumpled foil and bake in a preheated oven, 400°F, for 15 minutes. Remove the foil and bake for a further 10 minutes. Take the pastry shell out of the oven and lower the oven temperature to 350°F.

3 Meanwhile, make the filling. Broil the bacon until crisp, then drain it on paper towels; crumble or cut the cooled bacon into pieces. Beat the cream and eggs in a bowl with the nutmeg and salt and pepper to taste. Sprinkle the bacon over the pastry shell and pour the cream and egg filling over the top.

4 Place the quiche pan on a baking sheet and bake for about 30–35 minutes, until the filling is just set and the pastry is golden brown. Serve the quiche warm or cold.

quiche lorraine

Pastry:

1½ cups all-purpose flour

¾ stick (⅓ cup) chilled butter, diced

1 egg yolk, beaten

1–2 tablespoons cold water

Filling:

6 oz. sliced bacon

1 cup light cream

2 eggs, beaten

pinch of grated nutmeg

salt and pepper

Serves 4–6

Preparation time: 20 minutes plus chilling

Cooking time: 55–60 minutes

leek & potato bake

1 Place the potatoes in a saucepan of salted, boiling water and parboil for 3 minutes. Drain and slice.

2 Place the leeks in a greased casserole and season to taste with pepper. Arrange the potatoes on the top and pour the cream over. Cover with foil and bake in a preheated oven, 375°F, for about 45 minutes, or until the potatoes are tender.

3 Sprinkle with the cheese and breadcrumbs and cook under a preheated broiler until the top is browned. Serve at once.

2½ lb. potatoes, peeled

1 lb. (around 4 medium) leeks, trimmed and sliced

⅔ cup light cream

½ cup grated Cheddar cheese

1 cup fresh breadcrumbs

salt and pepper

Serves 6
Preparation time: 20 minutes
Cooking time: 50 minutes

■ This makes a great brunch or late supper dish.

classic hamburgers ●

crusty shepherd's pie ●

grilled italian sausages with mushrooms and polenta ●

farmhouse bake ●

beef & guinness pie ●

chile con carne ●

toad in the hole ●

carbonnade of beef ●

beef cobbler ●

goulash ●

braised ham ●

cassoulet ●

lancashire hot pots ●

steak & kidney pie ●

lamb tagine ●

lamb dhansak ●

meat dishes

classic hamburgers

1 In a large bowl, combine the ground steak, Worcestershire sauce, and grated onion. Season to taste and mix well. Form the mixture into 4 round flat patties.

2 Heat a large frying pan. If the meat is very lean, you may need to lightly oil the pan. Fry the burgers for 2–3 minutes on each side. Depending on how thick they are, you may need to cook them a bit longer, according to personal taste.

3 Serve on toasted hamburger buns or large rolls with onion rings, tomato slices, salad leaves, or your choice of toppings.

1 lb. ground beef chuck steak

3 tablespoons Worcestershire sauce

¼ cup grated onion

oil, for frying

salt and pepper

To Garnish:

sesame seed rolls or hamburger buns, toasted

onion rings

tomato slices

lettuce or other salad leaves

Makes 4
Preparation time: 10 minutes
Cooking time: 4–6 minutes

crusty shepherd's pie

1 Heat the oil in a frying pan, add the bacon and onion, and fry for 5 minutes, until softened. Add the lamb and fry, stirring, until evenly browned. Stir in the herbs, wine, and tomato purée, and season. Bring to a boil, then lower the heat and simmer, uncovered, for 25 minutes, until the lamb is tender and the sauce has thickened.

2 To make the scone topping, put the flour in a bowl and add salt and pepper to taste. Rub in the diced butter until the mixture resembles fine breadcrumbs. Stir in the mustard and two-thirds of the cheese, then add enough milk to make a soft dough.

3 Knead the dough briefly on a lightly floured surface, then roll out to a thickness of ½ inch. Using a 2-inch cookie cutter, press out as many 2-inch scones as you can. Reroll the leftover trimmings and press out more rounds. Transfer the meat mixture to a greased 1½-quart casserole. Arrange the scones over the top, brush with milk, and sprinkle with the remaining cheese. Bake in a preheated oven, 400°F, for about 25 minutes, until the topping is golden brown. Serve hot.

■ As an alternative, you can use ground beef instead of lamb

1 tablespoon olive oil

8 slices bacon, chopped

1 onion, chopped

1 lb. ground lamb

1 teaspoon dried oregano

2 tablespoons chopped parsley

⅔ cup red wine

a 14-oz. can tomato purée

salt and pepper

Scone Topping:

2 cups self-rising flour

½ stick (¼ cup) chilled butter, diced

2 teaspoons whole-grain mustard

1 cup grated sharp Cheddar cheese

½ cup milk

Serves 4–6

Preparation time: 20 minutes

Cooking time: 55 minutes

grilled italian sausages with mushrooms and polenta

1 To make the polenta, bring the water and salt to a boil in a large saucepan. Reduce the heat slightly and add the cornmeal in a thin stream, beating all the time. Cook, stirring constantly, for 20–30 minutes, until the mixture comes away from the sides of the pan. Tip the polenta onto a board or baking sheet. Leave to cool. Cut into thick slices, brush with olive oil, and set aside.

2 To prepare the mushrooms, remove the stalks and brush the caps all over with the reserved oil from the tomatoes. Finely chop the stalks and place in a bowl with the chopped sun-dried tomatoes, cheese, and pine nuts. Add salt and pepper to taste and mix to combine. Stuff the mushroom caps with this mixture.

3 Place 2 stuffed mushrooms on a piece of foil large enough to enclose them, bring up the edges, and seal well. Repeat with the remaining mushrooms.

4 Cook the sausages, polenta slices, and mushroom parcels on an oiled grill over hot coals for 15–20 minutes, or until the sausages are cooked, the mushrooms are tender, and the polenta is lightly crisp on the outside. Serve at once.

8 large cremini mushrooms

8 sun-dried tomato halves packed in oil, chopped, with 4 tablespoons oil reserved

½ lb. Gorgonzola or dolcelatte cheese, crumbled

⅓ cup pine nuts, toasted

8 Italian sausages or other good-quality sausages

Polenta:

3 cups water

1 teaspoon salt

1½ cups cornmeal

2 tablespoons olive oil

Serves 4
Preparation time: 20 minutes
Cooking time: 35–50 minutes

■ To toast pine nuts, dry-fry them in a hot frying pan, stirring constantly, until they become a golden brown color.

1 Fry the bacon in a nonstick frying pan until cooked and beginning to brown. Remove from the pan, pour off the bacon fat, and add the butter. Fry the onion and mushrooms until cooked and beginning to color.

2 Cut the potatoes into wedges and arrange with the fried bacon, mushrooms, and onions in an oval, 1-quart casserole. Season to taste and add the chopped parsley.

3 Pour the cream over it and cover with the grated Cheddar. Bake in a preheated oven, 350°F, for 20–30 minutes until crisp and golden on the top and very hot. Serve with broiled tomatoes, if you like.

around 16 slices bacon, cut into strips

1 tablespoon butter

1 large onion, finely chopped

1½ cups sliced mushrooms

6 potatoes, boiled

1 tablespoon chopped parsley

⅔ cup heavy cream

1 cup grated Cheddar cheese

salt and pepper

Serves 4	
Preparation time: 20 minutes	
Cooking time: about 30–40 minutes	

farmhouse bake

■ To make a pasta supper dish with the same rich, comforting flavors, substitute the potato wedges with 12 oz. dried macaroni or penne, boiled until just tender. Serve with a crisp green salad.

beef &
guinness pie

1 Heat the oil in a large pan, add the beef and fry until browned. Add the onions and celery and fry for 5 minutes. Stir in the flour and cook for 1 minute. Gradually stir in the Guinness and stock until the liquid is thickened. Stir in the remaining ingredients and season. Cover the pan and cook for 1½ hours until tender. Pour into a 1½-quart casserole and allow to cool slightly. Remove the bay leaves.

2 To make the pastry, mix the flour with a little salt in a bowl. Stir in the walnuts and mustard seeds. Add the butter and rub in with your fingertips until the mixture resembles breadcrumbs. Stir in enough cold water, about 2–3 tablespoons, to make a firm dough. Turn out onto a floured surface and knead briefly. Roll out to 2 inches larger than the casserole; cut off a strip 1 inch wide all around. Dampen the rim of the dish with water and press the pastry strip on top. Dampen the strip and cover with the pastry lid.

3 Decorate the pie by pinching the edges of the pastry between your thumb and finger. Make a small hole in the center to allow the steam to escape. Bake in a preheated oven, 375°F, for 35–40 minutes until crisp and golden brown.

2 tablespoons oil

2 lb. lean beef stewing meat, cubed

2 onions, thinly sliced

2 celery stalks, chopped

2 tablespoons all-purpose flour

2 cups Guinness

⅔ cup beef stock

2 teaspoons brown sugar

2 bay leaves

2 teaspoons Worcestershire sauce

1 tablespoon tomato paste

¾ cup (around 12) pitted prunes

salt and pepper

Pastry:

1½ cups all-purpose flour

¼ cup finely chopped walnuts

1 teaspoon mustard seeds

1 stick (½ cup) chilled butter, diced

Serves 6
Preparation time: 25 minutes plus chilling
Cooking time: 2–2¼ hours

chile con carne

1 Put the drained beans into a pot of cold water, bring to a boil, and boil rapidly for 10 minutes, then drain.

2 Heat the oil in a flameproof casserole, add the beef and cook, turning frequently, until browned. Add the onion and green chile and cook for 2–3 minutes. Add the oregano, cumin, pepper flakes, tomatoes and their juice, stock, and beans to the casserole and bring to a boil.

3 Cover the casserole and put it into a preheated oven, 325°F. Cook for 1½ hours, or until the beef and beans are tender. Taste and adjust the seasoning, if necessary, before serving.

1 cup pinto beans, soaked overnight

2 tablespoons oil

1¼ lb. chuck steak, finely diced

1 onion, chopped

1 small green chile, seeded and chopped

1 teaspoon dried oregano

1 tablespoon ground cumin

½ teaspoon crushed red pepper flakes

a 14-oz. can chopped tomatoes

1¼ cups beef stock

salt and pepper

Serves 4

Preparation time: 15 minutes plus soaking

Cooking time: 1¾ hours

2 cups all-purpose flour, sifted

1 teaspoon salt

2 large eggs, beaten

2½ cups milk

¼ cup pan drippings or lard

12 lightly broiled sausages

Serves 6

Preparation time: 15 minutes plus standing

Cooking time: 35–40 minutes

1 Put the flour and salt into a bowl and make a well in the center. Add the beaten eggs and half the milk and mix to a smooth paste, beating for at least 5 minutes. Add the remaining milk and beat again, then thin with cold water to the consistency of thick cream. Let the batter stand for about 30 minutes.

2 Heat the sausages and their drippings in a baking pan. The fat should be so hot that when the batter is poured in it sizzles. With your fingers, add a few drops of cold water to the batter and stir with a fork.

3 Pour the batter into the hot fat, then put immediately in a preheated oven, 425°F, and cook for 35–40 minutes. Do not open the oven door until the minimum cooking time has elapsed. The pudding is ready when the top is golden brown and crisp and the center is cooked, but still creamy.

toad in the hole

carbonnade of beef

1 Toss the meat in seasoned flour until well coated. Set aside any remaining flour. Melt the butter and oil in a frying pan, add the bacon and fry gently until browned. Transfer to a casserole. Add the onions to the frying pan and fry gently; then add the meat and brown it on both sides. Transfer the onions and meat to the casserole.

2 Sprinkle the reserved flour into the pan, add the ale, stock, and 1 teaspoon of the French mustard, and scrape the juices from the sides of the pan into the mixture. Stir together, season with salt and pepper, then pour over the meat in the casserole. Add the bouquet garni and parsley.

3 Put the covered casserole in a preheated oven, 350°F, and cook for 1½ hours, or until tender. Remove the bouquet garni, taste and adjust seasoning and consistency, if necessary. Place the slices of French bread, spread with the remaining mustard, on top of the meat and return the casserole, uncovered, to the oven for a further 15–20 minutes, or until the bread is golden brown. Serve at once.

1½ lb. chuck or round steak, trimmed and cut into 2-inch slices

1 tablespoon all-purpose flour, seasoned

½ stick (¼ cup) butter

1 tablespoon oil

4–5 slices bacon, diced

3 large onions, thinly sliced

1¼ cups brown ale or beer

1¼ cups beef stock

5 teaspoons French mustard

1 bouquet garni

2 tablespoons chopped parsley

8 slices French bread

salt and pepper

Serves 4

Preparation time: 25 minutes

Cooking time: 1¾–2 hours

1 Heat 2 tablespoons of the oil in a flameproof casserole. Toss the meat in the flour and fry in the oil over a high heat until golden brown. Reduce the heat, add the remaining oil and the vegetables and fry gently for a few minutes. Add the bay leaf, stock, and salt and pepper to taste, and bring to a boil. Cover the casserole, transfer it to a preheated oven, 350°F, and cook for 1 hour.

2 Meanwhile, make the scone topping: sift the flour and salt into a bowl, then rub in the fat until the mixture resembles fine breadcrumbs. Add the herbs and mix with the egg and milk to a soft dough. Roll out on a floured board to ½ inch thick and cut into rounds or small triangles.

3 Remove the casserole from the oven, taste and adjust the seasoning, and remove the bay leaf. Increase the temperature to 425°F and arrange the scones on top of the meat. Return the casserole, uncovered, to the oven for 15 minutes, or until the scone topping is golden brown.

4 tablespoons oil

1 lb. beef stewing meat, trimmed and cut into small cubes

1 tablespoon seasoned flour

2 onions, diced

2 carrots, diced

1 small turnip, diced

1 bay leaf

2 cups beef stock

salt and pepper

Scone Topping:

1 cup self-rising flour

¼ teaspoon salt

½ stick (¼ cup) butter

¼ teaspoon mixed herbs

1 egg

2 tablespoons milk

Serves 4
Preparation time: 30 minutes
Cooking time: 1½ hours

beef cobbler

1 Heat the oil in a frying pan and fry the meat until brown on all sides. Reduce the heat and sprinkle the paprika and flour over the meat, turning it to absorb the flour. After about 2–3 minutes pour the stock into the frying pan and stir gently. Add the meat and stock to a casserole.

2 Rinse the pan, melt the butter in it and sweat the onions and carrots gently. Add the herbs, tomatoes, tomato paste, lemon juice, diced potato, and salt and pepper to taste.

3 Pour the tomato mixture over the meat in the casserole and cook, covered, in a preheated oven, 325°F, for 1 hour. Add the onions and return for a further 45 minutes. Before serving the casserole, remove the bay leaf, taste and adjust the seasoning, stir in the sour cream, and garnish with parsley.

2 tablespoons oil

1 lb. beef stewing meat, cubed

2 teaspoons paprika

2 teaspoons flour

1¼ cups stock

2 tablespoons butter

1 cup diced onions

1½ cups diced carrots

1 bay leaf

a good pinch of thyme

a 14-oz. can tomatoes, with their juice

1 tablespoon tomato paste

1 teaspoon lemon juice

1 potato, diced

8 small onions

1 tablespoon sour cream

salt and pepper

finely chopped parsley, to garnish

Serves 4
Preparation time: 10–15 minutes
Cooking time: 2 hours

goulash

braised ham

1 Place the ham in a casserole, pour in the pale ale, season with pepper and cook, covered, in a preheated oven, 350°F, for 40 minutes.

2 Remove the ham from the casserole and discard half the ale. Cut away the skin from the ham and score the fat diagonally. Mix together the honey, sugar, and dry mustard, and rub over the ham. Stud cloves into the ham surface in a diamond pattern and return the ham and remaining ale to the casserole.

3 Increase the oven temperature to 400°F and cook the ham, uncovered, for another 30 minutes, basting it every 10 minutes. Serve garnished with wedges of orange and watercress.

2 lb. smoked ham rump portion (or butt half)

1¼ cups pale ale or beer

2 tablespoons honey

¼ cup light brown sugar

1 teaspoon dry mustard

12 cloves

pepper

To Garnish:

orange wedges

watercress

Serves 4
Preparation time: 15 minutes plus soaking
Cooking time: 1 hour 10 minutes

cassoulet

1 cup dried navy beans, soaked overnight

3 cups beef stock

¼ lb. fresh pork rind, diced

8 garlic cloves, peeled

1 carrot, trimmed and lightly scraped

1 onion, studded with 4 cloves

2 tablespoons oil

¼ lb. lean pork, cubed

¼ lb. salt pork, cubed

¾ lb. boned lamb shoulder, cubed

2 onions, thinly sliced

a 14-oz. can tomatoes, with their juice

1 bouquet garni

¾ lb. garlic sausage, cut into 2-inch lengths

2 cups fresh breadcrumbs

salt and pepper

2 tablespoons chopped parsley, to garnish

Serves 4
Preparation time: 30 minutes plus soaking
Cooking time: 5 hours

1 Drain the soaked beans and put them into a large saucepan with the stock, pork rind, 4 whole garlic cloves, the carrot, and the onion stuck with cloves. Cover, bring slowly to a boil, and simmer for 1 hour. Strain off the liquid and set it aside. Discard the carrot, onion, and garlic. Put the beans and pork rind into a deep casserole.

2 Heat the oil in a large frying pan, add the pork, salt pork, and lamb, and brown on all sides. Remove from the pan and add to the beans. Fry the sliced onions gently in the fat until softened. Stir in the tomatoes, the remaining garlic, crushed, the bean cooking liquid, the bouquet garni, and salt and pepper to taste. Bring to a boil and pour over the beans.

3 Mix all the ingredients together, then cover the casserole and cook in a preheated oven, 325°F, for 2½ hours. Remove the lid and carefully stir in the sausage. Taste and adjust the seasoning, if necessary. Sprinkle the crumbs evenly over the top and return to the oven, uncovered. Cook for a further 1 hour. The fat will rise to the surface to turn the crumbs into a crisp golden topping. Garnish with parsley.

■ Do not allow the cassoulet to get too dry during cooking; add a little more stock, if necessary. The final dish should have a creamy consistency.

1 Have ready 6 ovenproof bowls, approximately 14 fl oz. in size. Slice the lamb into 24 pieces. Heat a little of the oil to smoking point in a frying pan. Quickly fry the lamb in small batches to seal and color the meat. Place 4 pieces in each bowl.

2 Brown the onions in the pan over a fairly fierce heat, adding a bit more oil, if necessary. Lift the onions out with a slotted spoon and divide among the bowls. Do the same with the celery, mushrooms, and barley.

3 Season each bowl lightly with salt and pepper. Pour over enough wine and broth to cover. Arrange the potatoes neatly in overlapping circles on top of each bowl and brush with melted butter. Cover the bowls and cook in a preheated oven, 325°F, for 1½ hours. Take off the lids, raise the temperature to 375°F and cook for a further 20–30 minutes, or until the potatoes are golden-brown.

3 lb. sirloin or butt end of leg of lamb, trimmed

2 tablespoons olive oil, for frying

24 pearl onions

3 inner stalks of celery, finely diced

18 button mushrooms

2 tablespoons barley

⅔ cup dry white wine

2 cups chicken broth

6 potatoes, totaling 1½ lb., thinly sliced

2 tablespoons butter, melted

salt and pepper

Serves 6

Preparation time: 30 minutes

Cooking time: about 2½ hours

lancashire hot pots

steak & kidney pie

1 Put the steak, kidney, onion, celery, and carrots in a large saucepan. Add the water, thyme, and soy sauce, with salt and pepper to taste. Bring to a boil, then lower the heat, cover, and simmer for about 1½ hours, until the meat is tender.

2 Taste and add more seasoning, if necessary. In a cup, make a paste of the cornstarch and a little water. Stir into the pan, cooking until the meat sauce is thickened and smooth. Stir in the parsley and leave to cool.

3 Roll out half the pastry on a lightly floured surface and line a 1-quart ovenproof dish or a 9-inch pie plate. Place the cooled meat mixture over the pastry. Position a pastry funnel in the middle of the pie. Dampen the edges of the pie with water. Roll out the remaining pastry, making a hole in the middle for the pastry funnel, and cover the pie. Trim the edges, then cut up the edges with a knife, and flute to seal and decorate.

4 Reroll the pastry trimmings and cut into leaves. Adhere them to the top of the pie with a little of the beaten egg. Brush the pie crust with more egg and bake in a preheated oven, 425°F, for 35–40 minutes until the pastry is crisp and golden brown.

1½ lb. beef stewing meat, cubed

½ lb. beef or veal kidney, cored and trimmed

1 large onion, chopped

1 celery stalk, chopped

2 carrots, chopped

1¼ cups water

½ teaspoon dried thyme

1 tablespoon soy sauce

1 tablespoon cornstarch

2 tablespoons chopped parsley

12 oz. puff pastry, thawed if frozen

salt and pepper

beaten egg, to glaze

Serves 6
Preparation time: 25 minutes plus cooling
Cooking time: about 2 hours 20 minutes

■ To make a fluted edge, place the forefinger of one hand in the inside edge of the pastry rim. Pinch the pastry around it with the thumb and forefinger of your other hand to make a pinched edge. Continue all around the edge of the pie.

lamb tagine

2 tablespoons oil

1¼ lb. lamb leg meat, diced

1 large onion, chopped

1 garlic clove, crushed

1 teaspoon ground ginger

1 teaspoon ground cinnamon

2 tablespoons all-purpose flour

1¼ cups lamb stock

1½ cups pitted prunes (around 24 prunes)

salt and pepper

1 tablespoon toasted sesame seeds, to garnish

Serves 4

Preparation time: 15 minutes

Cooking time: 1 hour 40 minutes

■ Traditionally, this Moroccan stew is cooked in a tagine, a round and shallow earthenware pot with a conical lid.

1 Heat the oil in a frying pan, add the meat, and cook until it is brown on all sides. Remove the meat from the pan with a slotted spoon and put into a casserole.

2 Fry the onion and garlic in the pan until soft, then add the spices and cook for 1 minute. Sprinkle the flour into the pan and cook for just 1 minute, then add the stock and season to taste. Bring to a boil, then pour it over the lamb. Cover the casserole, and cook for 1 hour in a preheated oven, 350°F. Add the prunes and cook for a further 30 minutes.

3 Transfer the lamb and prunes to a warmed serving dish and sprinkle with the sesame seeds before serving.

lamb dhansak

1 Heat the oil in a large frying pan and fry the onions, pepper, zucchini, and garlic until soft. Add the curry powder paste and spices, and fry for 1–2 minutes, then add the lamb. Fry over a moderate heat to seal and brown the lamb on all sides.

2 Add the tomatoes and lamb stock or water and bring to a boil. Transfer to an ovenproof casserole and put in a preheated oven, 375°F, for 30 minutes.

3 Add the chopped cilantro, sugar, garam masala, drained lentils, and salt to taste, with a little water to moisten, if necessary. Return the casserole to the oven and cook for a further 40 minutes. Spoon off any excess oil before serving the dish and garnish with parsley sprigs.

¼ cup oil

2 onions, diced

1 yellow bell pepper, chopped

1 small zucchini, chopped

2 garlic cloves, chopped

2 tablespoons curry powder

2 tablespoons mild curry paste

2 tablespoons ground coriander

1 teaspoon ground cumin

1 lb. lamb leg meat, diced

a 14-oz. can chopped tomatoes with their juice

1¼ cups lamb stock or water

1 tablespoon chopped cilantro

1 tablespoon brown sugar

1 tablespoon garam masala or curry powder

a 13-oz. can red lentils, rinsed and drained

salt

parsley, to garnish

Serves 4
Preparation time: 20 minutes
Cooking time: 1½ hours

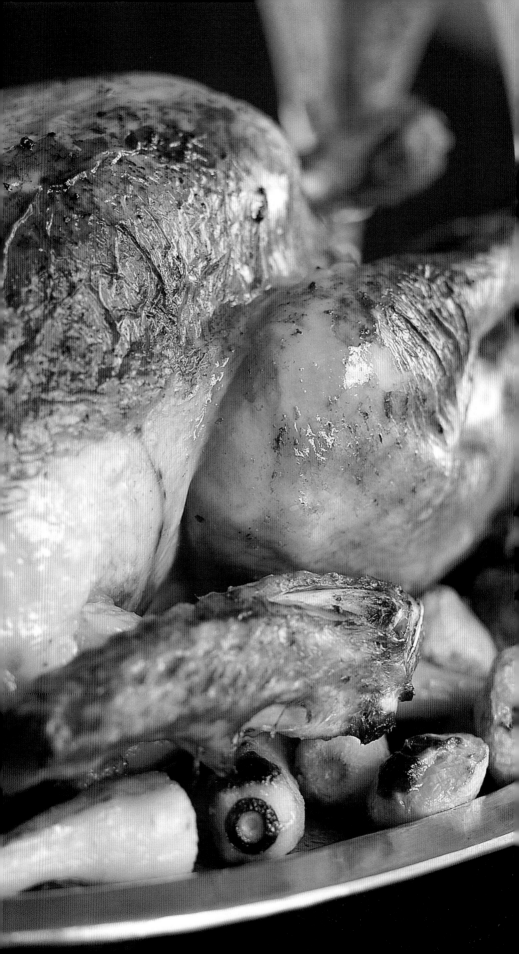

chicken & poultry dishes

1 stick (½ cup) butter

3 large onions, finely sliced

10 peppercorns

10 cardamom pods

a 2-inch piece cinnamon stick

a 2-inch piece fresh ginger root, chopped

2 garlic cloves, finely chopped

1 teaspoon chili powder

2 teaspoons paprika

3 lb. chicken pieces, skinned

1 cup plain yogurt

salt

To Garnish:

lime wedges

parsley sprigs

1 Melt the butter in a deep, lidded frying pan or wok. Add the onions, peppercorns, cardamom pods, and cinnamon and fry until the onions are golden. Add the ginger, garlic, chili powder, paprika, and salt to taste, and fry for 2 minutes, stirring occasionally.

2 Add the chicken pieces and fry until browned. Gradually add the yogurt, stirring constantly. Cover and cook for about 30 minutes. Serve hot, garnished with lime wedges and parsley sprigs.

Serves 6	
Preparation time: 10 minutes	
Cooking time: about 40 minutes	

kashmiri chicken

chicken korma

1   Cook the onion and garlic gently in the butter or ghee in a large pan until soft. Add the saffron, coriander, chili powder, and half the water and cook for 3 minutes, stirring constantly.

2   Add the chicken and simmer for 20 minutes, covered. When the liquid has evaporated, continue to cook, stirring, until the chicken is golden brown.

3   Add the yogurt, cream, cumin, cloves, cardamom, poppy seeds, and sesame seeds, and season to taste. Add the remaining water, cover the pan, and simmer gently until the chicken is tender—about 10 minutes. Add more water if the sauce becomes too dry. Transfer to a warmed serving dish and garnish with parsley and pistachios. Serve hot.

1 onion, finely sliced

2 garlic cloves, crushed

1 stick (½ cup) butter or ghee

½ teaspoon saffron threads

3 teaspoons ground coriander

½ teaspoon ground chili powder

1¼ cups water

1½ lb. skinless chicken breast, cut into chunks

¼ cup plain yogurt

½ cup light cream

1 teaspoon white cumin seeds

10 cloves

4 brown cardamom seeds

1 teaspoon poppy seeds

1 teaspoon sesame seeds

salt and pepper

To Garnish:

parsley sprigs

2 tablespoons roughly chopped pistachios

Serves 4
Preparation time: 15 minutes
Cooking time: 45 minutes

chicken kiev

1 Put the chicken breasts between 2 sheets of wax paper and pound until thin, using a rolling pin. Cut the garlic butter into 4 sticks. Put 1 stick in the center of each chicken breast, then roll the chicken around the stick, folding in the sides so the butter is completely enclosed. If necessary, secure with toothpicks.

2 Season the flour and spread out on one plate, the beaten eggs on a second plate, and the breadcrumbs on a third. Coat the chicken breasts first in the seasoned flour, then in the beaten eggs, and then in the breadcrumbs. Press the breadcrumbs on firmly so that they stick. Repeat to give a second coating of egg and breadcrumbs (this helps to insulate the garlic butter so that the heat from the oil does not penetrate too early and melt the butter before the chicken is cooked). Chill for at least 1 hour.

3 Heat the oil in a deep-fat fryer to 350–375°F, or until a cube of bread browns in 30 seconds. Carefully lower the chicken parcels into the hot oil and deep-fry for 7–10 minutes, or until the breadcrumbs are golden brown and crisp on all sides; turn the chicken very carefully halfway through. Lift out the chicken with a slotted spoon and drain on paper towels. Remove and discard the toothpicks. Serve hot with a mixed green salad.

4 large skinless, boneless chicken breasts

½ cup garlic butter (see below)

4 teaspoons all-purpose flour

2 eggs, beaten

4 cups dry white breadcrumbs

oil, for deep-frying

salt and pepper

mixed green salad, to serve

Serves 4
Preparation time: 30 minutes plus freezing and chilling
Cooking time: 7–10 minutes

■ For garlic butter, beat 4 crushed garlic cloves and 2 tablespoons chopped fresh parsley into ½ cup softened unsalted butter. Form into a wedge, wrap in wax paper, and freeze for at least 1 hour, until firm.

chicken marengo

1 Sprinkle the chicken with salt and pepper. Melt half of the butter in a pan, add the chicken, and brown on all sides. Transfer to a casserole. Warm the brandy, pour it over the chicken, and ignite. When the flames have died down, set the dish aside.

2 Add the remaining butter to the pan and then add the onion and garlic. Fry gently until lightly colored. Add the flour to the onions and cook for 1 minute. Add the tomatoes, wine, and tomato paste and bring to a boil. Add the mushrooms, taste, and adjust the seasoning, if necessary, and simmer for 2 minutes. Pour the sauce over the chicken and cover the casserole. Cook in a preheated oven, 350°F, for about 45–50 minutes, or until tender.

3 To garnish, lightly fry the crayfish or shrimp in butter. Arrange the chicken on plates, spoon the sauce over it, and garnish with the crayfish or shrimp, eggs, and walnuts or olives.

4 lb. chicken, cut into 8 pieces, skin removed

½ stick (¼ cup) butter

2 tablespoons brandy

1 onion, sliced

1–2 garlic cloves, crushed

2 tablespoons flour

a 14-oz. can tomatoes, puréed or very finely chopped

⅔ cup dry white wine

1 tablespoon tomato paste

¼ lb. button mushrooms, trimmed and halved

salt and pepper

To Garnish:

4 crayfish or 8 jumbo shrimp

2 tablespoons butter

2 hard-boiled eggs, shelled and quartered

a few pickled walnut slices or black olives

Serves 4
Preparation time: 20 minutes
Cooking time: 1 hour 10 minutes

chicken véronique

1 Sprinkle the chicken pieces lightly with salt and pepper. Heat the butter and oil in a pan, add the chicken, and fry until lightly browned all over. Transfer to a casserole.

2 Stir the flour into the pan juices, then add the wine and broth and bring to a boil. Add the lemon zest and juice and pour it over the chicken. Add the bay leaf. Cover the casserole and cook in a preheated oven, 350°F, for 40 minutes.

3 Blend the cream with the egg yolk, add some of the sauce from the casserole, then stir it back into the casserole with the grapes. Replace the lid and return it to the oven for 15 minutes. Discard the bay leaf and serve the chicken garnished with small bunches of grapes.

4 skinless, part-boned chicken breasts

2 tablespoons butter

1 tablespoon oil

2 tablespoons all-purpose flour

⅔ cup white wine

⅔ cup chicken broth

grated zest of ½ lemon

1 tablespoon lemon juice

1 bay leaf

⅔ cup light cream

1 egg yolk

½ cup seedless green grapes, peeled and halved, plus extra to garnish

salt and pepper

Serves 4
Preparation time: 15 minutes
Cooking time: 1 hour

1 Remove the giblets from the chicken and set aside for the gravy stock. Put 1 lemon and the bouquet garni inside the chicken cavity and truss the chicken securely. Place the chicken in an oiled roasting pan, pour the olive oil over it, and season. Place the pan in a preheated oven, 350°F, and roast for 1½–1¾ hours, or until the chicken is tender.

2 Prepare the bread sauce about 15 minutes before the chicken is cooked. Pour the milk into a pan and add the onion, cloves, and bay leaves. Heat until the milk has almost reached boiling point. Stir in the breadcrumbs and butter. Remove from the heat and leave for 5 minutes. Add nutmeg and salt to taste.

3 Remove the chicken from the oven and place it on a serving dish. Pour off all but 2 tablespoons of fat from the pan, leaving the residue. Add the flour to the pan and stir over a low heat until bubbling and golden. Gradually stir in the stock or wine. Season and simmer for 5 minutes. Serve hot with the sauce, gravy, and lemon wedges.

3–4 lb. oven-ready chicken with giblets

2 lemons

1 bouquet garni

¼ cup olive oil

salt and pepper

Bread Sauce:

2½ cups milk

1 small onion, grated

pinch of ground cloves

pinch of ground bay leaves

3 cups fresh white breadcrumbs

2 tablespoons butter

pinch of grated nutmeg

Gravy:

2 tablespoons all-purpose flour

1¼ cups giblet stock or wine

Serves 6
Preparation time: 30 minutes
Cooking time: 1½–1¾ hours

roast chicken with bread sauce & gravy

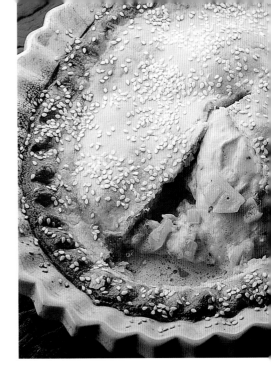

1. Season the flour with salt and pepper and use to toss the chicken until coated. Melt the butter and oil in a frying pan, add the onions, and fry for 5 minutes, or until softened and browned. Remove the onions from the pan and set aside. Add the chicken to the pan and fry for about 10 minutes, or until browned. Using a slotted spoon, transfer the chicken to a 1½-quart casserole or pie dish. Sprinkle the onions over the top.

2. Stir any remaining flour into the pan and cook for 1 minute. Gradually add the broth, stirring until the sauce is thick and smooth, scraping the base of the pan to incorporate any sediment. Stir in the lemon juice and let it bubble briefly. Stir in the heavy cream and parsley. Bring to a boil. Taste and adjust the seasoning, if necessary, then pour the sauce over the chicken.

3. Roll out your prepared pastry dough to measure 2 inches larger than the pie dish. Cut off a 1-inch strip all around. Dampen the edge of the dish and attach the strip. Brush the strip with water and cover the pie with the remaining pastry. Pinch the edges of the pastry together and make a hole to allow the steam to escape. Brush the pastry with beaten egg or milk and sprinkle with sesame seeds. Bake in a preheated oven, 400°F, for 30 minutes, then reduce the oven temperature to 350°F, and bake for a further 45 minutes. Cover with foil if the pastry becomes too brown. Serve the pie hot.

chicken pot pie

1 tablespoon all-purpose flour

8–10 boneless chicken thighs (about 1¼ lb. total weight)

2 tablespoons butter

1 tablespoon olive oil

2 onions, chopped

1¼ cups chicken broth

2 tablespoons lemon juice

⅔ cup heavy cream

1 bunch parsley, chopped

1 recipe of shortcrust pastry dough, omitting the sugar (see page 84)

beaten egg or milk, to glaze

1 tablespoon sesame seeds

salt and pepper

Serves 4–6

Preparation time: 30 minutes

Cooking time: 1½ hours

crispy orange duck

1 Dry the duckling thoroughly, inside and out with paper towels, then season the cavity. Tuck the tarragon and 4 of the kumquats inside the duckling, then place it on a rack over a roasting pan. With a needle, prick the duckling in several places to release the fat during cooking. Rub the skin with salt and roast it in a preheated oven, 375°F, for 1½ hours, or until the skin is crisp and golden.

2 A few minutes before the duckling is cooked, cut the remaining kumquats in half and place them in a pan with the orange juice, sherry, and honey. Bring to a boil and simmer gently for about 2 minutes, stirring constantly.

3 To serve, carve the duckling into 4 quarters, place on a warmed serving dish, spoon the kumquats over it, and serve with the green beans.

a 4-lb. duckling

3 tarragon sprigs

½ lb. kumquats

1 tablespoon orange juice

3 tablespoons sherry

1 tablespoon honey

salt and pepper

green beans, to serve

Serves 4
Preparation time: 15 minutes
Cooking time: about 1½ hours

■ Kumquats are oval-shaped, small fruits with a distinctive citrus flavor. They do not need to be peeled; they can be eaten whole, skin and all.

1 First make the stuffing. Heat the oil in a pan and fry the onion until soft. Stir in the walnuts, breadcrumbs, lemon zest, parsley and marjoram, and season to taste. Bind with the egg.

2 Prick the duck all over with a fine skewer. Fill the body cavity with the stuffing. Truss the duck and set on a wire rack in a roasting pan. Mix the lemon juice and honey and brush the mixture over the duck. Season well and cook in a preheated oven, 425°F, for 10 minutes, then reduce the heat to 375°F, and cook for a further 2–2½ hours, depending on the size, and allowing about 10–15 minutes resting time at the end.

3 Baste frequently during cooking, brushing with any remaining honey mixture. Remove from the oven and drain off all but 1 tablespoon of fat from the pan. Stir in the flour, blending with the cooking juices, add the stock, and boil to thicken for the gravy. Garnish with watercress and serve with roasted root vegetables.

a 5–6-lb. duckling

2 tablespoons lemon juice

2 tablespoons clover honey

2 tablespoons all-purpose flour

1¼ cups duck or chicken stock

salt and pepper

watercress, to garnish

Walnut Stuffing:

1 tablespoon oil

1 onion, finely chopped

¾ cup chopped walnuts

4 cups fresh white breadcrumbs

grated zest of 1 lemon

1 tablespoon chopped parsley

1 teaspoon chopped marjoram

1 egg, beaten

Serves 4
Preparation time: 20 minutes
Cooking time: 2¼–2¾ hours

roast honey duck with walnut stuffing

coq au vin

1 Melt half of the butter in a flameproof casserole, add the bacon and onions, and cook gently until the onions begin to color. Transfer to a plate.

2 Add the quartered chicken to the casserole and brown on all sides. Warm the brandy, pour it over the chicken, and set alight. When the flames have died down, return the bacon and onions to the casserole. Heat the wine in a saucepan and pour it over the chicken. Season to taste with salt and pepper. Stir in the garlic, bouquet garni, and nutmeg. Cover the casserole and cook in a preheated oven, 350°F, for 1 hour.

3 Add the mushrooms to the casserole and stir; re-cover and cook for a further 15 minutes. Remove the bouquet garni. Mix the flour and the remaining butter to a paste and whisk it into the sauce in small pieces. Bring just to a boil, stirring. Adjust the seasoning and garnish with the croûtons and parsley.

½ stick (¼ cup) butter

¼ lb. thick-cut bacon, blanched and diced

12 baby onions or shallots

a 3-lb. roasting chicken, quartered

2 tablespoons brandy

1 bottle dry red wine

2 garlic cloves, crushed

1 bouquet garni

½ teaspoon grated nutmeg

½ lb. small button mushrooms

4 teaspoons all-purpose flour

salt and pepper

To Garnish:

heart-shaped fried croûtons (toasts)

chopped parsley

Serves 4
Preparation time: 40 minutes
Cooking time: 1½ hours

60

roast turkey

1 Remove the giblets from the turkey and use them to make stock and the stuffing. Wash the inside of the turkey and dry thoroughly with paper towels. Pack the stuffing loosely into the neck of the bird. (Don't stuff the body cavity because this may prevent the bird from cooking through.)

2 Place the onion in the body cavity, season to taste, and sew the opening closed. Once you have trussed the turkey, place it in a large roasting pan and rub it all over with butter. Add the oil to the pan and season the outside of the turkey with salt and pepper.

3 Roast in a preheated oven, 350°F, for 3–3¼ hours, basting from time to time. Cover with foil when sufficiently browned. Check if it is ready by inserting a skewer into the thickest part of the thigh; the juices should run clear. If they are pink, cook for a further 15 minutes and test again. Repeat, as necessary.

4 Transfer the turkey to a large dish. Pour off the fat from the juices, and use if making gravy. Arrange the turkey on a warmed serving platter and serve with gravy, bread sauce, and an assortment of seasonal vegetables.

a 10–12-lb. turkey, with giblets
Pecan Stuffing (see page 61)
1 small onion, cut in half
3 tablespoons butter, softened
2 tablespoons vegetable oil
salt and pepper

Serves 8

Preparation time: 20 minutes

Cooking time: 3–3¼ hours

■ Traditional English accompaniments to roast turkey are Bread Sauce (see page 54), roast potatoes, and roasted parsnips. The vegetables can be roasted in the turkey juices around the bird, if you like. Remember to allow 10-15 minutes resting time before carving, to let the meat relax. Carving straight from the oven can result in tough meat.

pecan stuffing

1 Put the heart and liver into a saucepan, and cover with water. Bring to a boil and simmer for 10 minutes. Chop the organ meat finely and set aside to cool.

2 Place the meat in a bowl and stir in the breadcrumbs, nuts, egg, spices, parsley, and celery salt.

3 Melt the butter in a saucepan, add the mushrooms and onion, and cook over a moderate heat, stirring frequently, for about 5 minutes or until softened. Stir this into the meat mixture, add the sherry, and season to taste.

heart and liver from the turkey

2 cups fresh breadcrumbs

½ cup finely chopped pecans

1 hardboiled egg, chopped

pinch of each of grated nutmeg, ground mace, and thyme

1 tablespoon chopped parsley

pinch of celery salt

3 tablespoons butter

¾ cup finely chopped mushrooms

1 small onion, chopped

2 tablespoons dry sherry

salt and pepper

Preparation time: 5 minutes
Cooking time: 15–20 minutes

fish & shellfish

salmon steaks
with orange sauce

1 Sprinkle the orange juice over the salmon steaks, season with pepper, and set aside at room temperature for at least 15 minutes.

2 Brush the rack of a broiler pan with oil. Brush the salmon steaks with half the melted butter and cook on the rack for 4 minutes under a preheated broiler. Turn the steaks over, brush them with the remaining butter, and broil for a further 5 minutes.

3 To make the sauce, put all the ingredients except the oil in a blender. Blend for 2–3 seconds. With the machine still running, pour in the oil slowly. Taste the sauce and adjust the seasoning, if necessary. Serve the salmon and orange sauce with orange wedges and a steamed green vegetable, such as asparagus.

2 tablespoons orange juice

4 salmon steaks, about ¼ lb. each

vegetable oil, for brushing

2 tablespoons butter, melted

orange wedges, to serve

salt and pepper

Orange Sauce:

1 egg

pinch of mustard powder

2 teaspoons grated orange zest

1 tablespoon orange juice

½ cup vegetable oil

Serves 4

Preparation time: 10 minutes plus marinating

Cooking time: 10 minutes

sole véronique

1 Place the sole fillets in a lightly oiled ovenproof dish. Surround them with the onion slices, bay leaf, parsley, fish stock, and season to taste.

2 Pour in the wine just to cover and bake in a preheated oven, 325°F, for up to 20 minutes, according to the thickness of the fillets. Transfer the fillets to a warmed serving dish and keep warm. Strain the cooking liquid into a pan and reduce it to 6 tablespoons.

3 To make the sauce, melt the butter in a saucepan, add the flour, and stir for 2 minutes over a low heat. Remove from the heat and gradually stir in the milk and reduced stock, and season with salt and pepper. Return the pan to a low heat, bring to a boil, and cook for 2–3 minutes, stirring constantly until the sauce thickens. Remove from the heat and stir in the heavy cream. Coat the fillets with this sauce and garnish with the grapes and sprigs of dill. Remove the bay leaf before serving. Serve at once with a selection of vegetables.

8 sole fillets, skinned and rolled

1 onion, sliced

1 bay leaf

a few parsley sprigs

⅔ cup fish stock

1–1¼ cups dry white wine

salt and pepper

Sauce:

2 tablespoons butter

2 tablespoons all-purpose flour

⅔ cup milk

⅔ cup heavy cream

To Garnish:

about 20 seedless red or green grapes, cut in half

dill sprigs

Serves 4
Preparation time: 15 minutes
Cooking time: about 40 minutes

1 Cook the wild rice in a large pot of boiling, salted water for about 40–45 minutes, or according to the package instructions, until tender.

2 Meanwhile, melt the butter in a large saucepan over medium heat, add the shallots, and cook for 3 minutes until soft. Add the wine, orange juice, orange zest, and red currant jelly, if using. Bring to a boil, then boil until reduced by half. Season with salt and pepper and add honey to taste. Cover the saucepan and keep warm.

3 Coat the sole fillets with the flour and season to taste. Heat the oil in a frying pan, add the sole fillets, in batches, and cook for 3 minutes on each side, or until cooked through. Remove from the pan and keep warm.

4 Drain the rice and stir in the orange segments. Spoon onto warmed serving plates and place the fish on top. Pour the sauce over the fish, garnish with parsley, and serve.

1 cup wild rice

2 tablespoons butter

4 shallots, finely chopped

1¼ cups dry white wine

1 cup orange juice

2 teaspoons grated orange zest

3 teaspoons red currant jelly (optional)

honey, to taste

8 lemon sole fillets

2 tablespoons flour

sunflower oil, for frying

2 oranges, peeled, and cut into segments

salt and pepper

parsley, to garnish

Serves 4
Preparation time: 10–15 minutes
Cooking time: 45 minutes

lemon sole with citrus & wild rice

tuna fish cakes

1 Mash the potatoes with the butter, then mix in the tuna, parsley, half the beaten egg, and salt and pepper to taste.

2 Chill the mixture for 20 minutes, then place on a floured surface, and shape into a roll. Cut into 8 slices and shape each into a flat patty, about 2½ inches in diameter. Dip them into the remaining egg, then coat with breadcrumbs.

3 Heat the oil in a frying pan, add the fish cakes in batches, and fry for 2–3 minutes on each side, or until golden brown and heated through. Garnish each fish cake with a parsley sprig. Serve with lemon wedges.

around 10 oz. potatoes, boiled

2 tablespoons butter

two 6-oz. cans tuna, drained and flaked

2 tablespoons chopped parsley

2 eggs, beaten

¾ cup dry breadcrumbs

oil, for frying

salt and pepper

parsley sprigs, to garnish

lemon wedges, to serve

Serves 4
Preparation time: 15 minutes plus chilling
Cooking time: about 20 minutes

■ These fish cakes are even more tasty when accompanied by a simple tomato sauce. Place a 14-oz. can chopped tomatoes, 1 crushed garlic clove, 3 tablespoons olive oil, and 1 teaspoon of sugar in a saucepan. Bring to a boil and simmer gently for 15 minutes. Season to taste with salt, pepper, and lemon juice.

four 1-inch-thick tuna steaks

Marinade:

2 tablespoons olive oil

1 tablespoon red wine vinegar

1 shallot, finely chopped

1 garlic clove, crushed

freshly ground black pepper

salade niçoise with hot grilled tuna

Salad:

3 hard-boiled eggs, quartered

6–8 lettuce leaves

2 tomatoes, sliced

10–12 slices peeled cucumber, seeded

4 green bell pepper rings

8 chicory leaves

8 watercress sprigs

1 small onion, sliced

8 black or green olives

8 anchovy fillets

1 tablespoon capers

1 Cut each piece of fish across the middle into 2 pieces. Mix the marinade ingredients together, then pour them over the fish, cover, and leave to marinate overnight.

2 Assemble the salad on 4 plates. Put all the dressing ingredients into a screw-top jar and shake until well mixed. Taste and adjust the seasoning. Drizzle some of the dressing over each salad.

3 Remove the fish from the marinade and sear under a hot broiler or in a lightly oiled frying pan. Baste with the marinade and cook for 2 minutes only on each side. Arrange the hot pieces of tuna on top of the salad and serve immediately.

■ If fresh tuna is not available, use halibut or swordfish pieces for this salad.

Dressing:

3 tablespoons olive oil

1½ tablespoons red wine vinegar

1 teaspoon French mustard

1 small garlic clove, finely chopped

Serves 4
Preparation time: 40 minutes plus marinating
Cooking time: 4 minutes

cheesy fish pie

1 Put the fish into a shallow pan with the bay leaf, peppercorns, and half of the milk. Bring to a boil and simmer, covered, for 15 minutes, or until the fish flakes easily. In another pan, heat the oil and fry the onions for 15 minutes, or until soft and lightly golden. Spoon into an ovenproof dish and arrange the fish on top. Strain the milk from the fish pan and set aside.

2 Put the potatoes in a saucepan, sprinkling each layer with a few slivers of garlic, some nutmeg, and salt and pepper. Cover with the remaining milk, bring to a boil, then simmer gently for about 8–10 minutes until they are just done.

3 Put 4 of the eggs into a small pan, cover with water, and boil for about 10 minutes until hard. Add the tomatoes to the oil that's left in the onion pan and stir-fry over a high heat for 2–3 minutes. Arrange the tomatoes on top of the fish and sprinkle with the dill.

4 Drain the potatoes, reserving the milk. Cool the eggs, then shell and slice them. Arrange the slices over the tomatoes, then cover with the potatoes. Beat the remaining 2 eggs well, then whisk in the 2 lots of milk. Pour this over the dish, adding extra milk, if necessary, so the liquid is level with the potatoes. Sprinkle the cheese over it. Cook in a preheated oven, 350°F, for 20 minutes. Garnish with dill sprigs and serve.

1 lb. skinless white fish fillets (e.g., cod or haddock)

1 bay leaf

6 white peppercorns

5 cups milk

2 tablespoons olive oil

2 large onions, finely sliced

1 lb. (about 4 small-to-medium) potatoes, finely sliced

1 garlic clove, sliced

pinch of grated nutmeg

6 large eggs

1 lb. (around 3 medium) tomatoes, peeled and finely sliced

½ teaspoon dried dill

½ cup grated Cheddar cheese

salt and pepper

dill sprigs, to garnish

Serves 6

Preparation time: 20–25 minutes

Cooking time: about 40 minutes

skate with black butter

1   Place the water, 2 tablespoons of the vinegar, the lemon zest, onion, peppercorns, carrot, and salt in a saucepan. Bring to a boil and simmer for 30 minutes, then remove from the heat and allow to cool (plunging the pan into a basin of very cold water will speed up this process).

2   Put the fish in one layer in a large flameproof pan. Strain the cooled bouillon over it and slowly bring to a boil. Allow to bubble for 5 seconds, then cook over the lowest possible heat—the liquid should barely simmer—for 12–15 minutes until the fish is cooked. Transfer the fish to a hot serving dish.

3   Melt the butter in a frying pan and cook over a medium heat until a deep golden color (despite the name, the butter should not turn black, as it would be burnt). Cook for a few seconds only, then pour it over the fish. Quickly pour the remaining vinegar into the pan and bring to a boil over a high heat. Stir in the capers and chopped parsley and pour this over the fish immediately. Garnish with parsley sprigs and serve hot.

5 cups cold water

4 tablespoons wine vinegar

a 2-inch piece of lemon zest

1 onion, sliced

12 white peppercorns, lightly crushed

1 carrot, sliced

¼ teaspoon finely ground sea salt

6 skate wings (about ½ lb. each), rinsed in cold water

1 stick (½ cup) unsalted butter

1 tablespoon capers, chopped

3 tablespoons finely chopped parsley

parsley sprigs, to garnish

Serves 6

Preparation time: 10 minutes plus cooling

Cooking time: 45 minutes

grilled fillet of sole with an herb crust

1 Roughly tear the bread into pieces, place in a food processor, and make into breadcrumbs. Put the breadcrumbs into a bowl with the herbs and mix together. Season with salt and add a squeeze of lemon juice. Stir in enough of the oil and melted butter to make the mixture moist.

2 Meanwhile, put the fish fillets, skin side down, on a sheet of greased foil on a broiler rack. Season to taste, dot with butter, and spread with the herb mixture. Place the fillets under a preheated broiler and cook for about 10 minutes, or until they are cooked through.

3 Arrange the fish fillets on top of the tomato slices, or on a bed of onions and tomatoes or other vegetables, and serve at once.

2 slices (around 3 oz.) sun-dried tomato bread

3 tablespoons finely chopped mixed parsley, tarragon, and chives

squeeze of lemon juice

3 tablespoons olive oil plus extra for greasing

2 tablespoons butter, melted

4 flounder or sole fillets

2 onions, thinly sliced

4 yellow tomatoes, thinly sliced

salt and pepper

Serves 2
Preparation time: 15 minutes
Cooking time: 10 minutes

shellfish paella

1 Clean the mussels, scrubbing them well and removing the beards. Discard any that are open. Cook in a little water in a large pot until they have opened. Discard any that have not opened. Set aside the cooking liquid. Shell the lobster, or skin and bone the monkfish, and cut up the flesh. Slice the squid into thin rings and slice the scallops. Slice the red and green peppers into thin strips and gently cook in 2 tablespoons of the olive oil. Remove from the pot and keep warm.

2 Add the sliced squid and scallops (and monkfish, if using) to the pot and turn them gently as they cook, then remove and keep warm. In a large paella dish or shallow pan, gently cook the onion in the remaining olive oil until transparent. Add the rice and fry gently for a few more minutes, then pour in the wine, fish stock, and reserved mussel liquid. Bring to a simmering point, add the saffron powder, and give a few careful stirs; then add the bay leaves.

3 After about 10–15 minutes, the rice, now a saffron yellow, should have absorbed the stock and you can stir in the peas. Then add the shrimp, all the reserved fish and shellfish, and the red and green peppers, and, again, give a few gentle stirs. Let the paella heat through, tasting and adjusting the seasoning, if necessary. Remove the bay leaves before serving.

2 quarts mussels

1 medium cooked lobster or ½ lb. monkfish

¾ lb. cleaned squid

12 scallops

1 red bell pepper, cored and seeded

1 green bell pepper, cored and seeded

6 tablespoons olive oil

2 large Spanish onions, finely chopped

4 cups long-grain rice

⅔ cup dry white wine

1 quart fish stock

2–3 teaspoons saffron powder

2 bay leaves

2 cups frozen peas

1 lb. peeled, cooked large shrimp

salt and pepper

Serves 8

Preparation time: 35 minutes

Cooking time: about 25 minutes

lobster thermidor

1 Lay the lobsters on their backs and, with a strong, sharp knife, cut in half lengthwise, taking care not to damage the shells. Otherwise, ask your fish seller to do this for you. Extract the meat from the body and claws. Reserve the lobster shells and oil them lightly. Chop up the lobster flesh and gently sauté it in a third of the butter for 4 minutes, turning all the time, then remove from the pan and keep warm.

2 Melt the remaining butter in a saucepan and gently cook the shallot, then add the flour and cook for 1–2 minutes. Remove from the heat and gradually stir in the wine and the stock. Return to low heat and bring to a boil, stirring constantly until thickened. Cook for 2–3 minutes. Add the mustard, salt and pepper to taste, and a little lemon juice, if you like.

3 Fold the lobster flesh into this sauce and pour the mixture into the lobster shells. Sprinkle the browned breadcrumbs over the mixture in the shells and brown under a preheated broiler until golden and bubbling. Sprinkle with the parsley and garnish with the lime twists and lemon geranium sprigs, if using.

2 cooked lobsters, each weighing about 1½ lb.

⅓ cup butter

1 shallot, finely chopped

½ cup all-purpose flour

¼ cup dry white wine

1¼ cups fish stock

1 teaspoon prepared English mustard

2 tablespoons lemon juice (optional)

¼ cup whole-wheat breadcrumbs, browned in a little butter

salt and pepper

To Garnish:

1 tablespoon chopped parsley

lime twists

lemon geranium sprigs (optional)

Serves 4
Preparation time: 20 minutes
Cooking time: 15 minutes

1 Scrub and clean all the mussels, removing any beards. Place the mussels, discarding any that are open, in a large pot with the shallots, onion, parsley, wine, and butter. Bring to a boil, cover, and simmer for about 5 minutes, shaking the pot occasionally, until the shells are open. Remove the mussels with a slotted spoon, and discard any mussels that do not open. Pile the mussels into a warmed serving bowl and keep hot.

2 Strain the cooking liquid into another pan. Bring to a boil and continue boiling for 1 minute. Season to taste, then pour the sauce over the mussels.

3 Garnish with parsley and serve with warm French bread.

moules marinière

■ To make the sauce richer, stir in 3 tablespoons of light cream just before serving. Do not allow the sauce to boil after the cream has been added.

2½ quarts mussels

2 shallots

1 onion, chopped

1 cup chopped parsley

1¼ cups dry white wine

½ stick (¼ cup) butter

salt and pepper

chopped parsley, to garnish

French bread, to serve

Serves 4
Preparation time: 20 minutes
Cooking time: 6 minutes

desserts
& baking

mocha
pots

1 Break the chocolate into a heatproof bowl. Add the butter and coffee powder and place the bowl over a pan of hot water. Heat gently until melted, being careful not to let the water in the pan boil. Beat in the egg yolks until smooth. Remove from heat and stir in the liqueur.

2 Whisk the egg whites until stiff and fold into the chocolate mixture. Spoon into 4 coffee cups or small glasses. Chill until set.

3 Just before serving, decorate each mocha pot with a rosette of whipped cream and crystallized violets, if using. Serve at once.

3 squares semi-sweet baking chocolate

2 tablespoons butter

1 tablespoon instant coffee powder

3 eggs, separated

1 tablespoon chocolate or coffee liqueur

To Decorate:

whipped cream

crystallized violet petals (optional)

Serves 4
Preparation time: 15 minutes plus chilling
Cooking time: 3 minutes

old english trifle

1 Cut the sponge cake in half horizontally, spread with jam, and sandwich it back together. (If using ladyfingers, spread the insides of them with jam and sandwich back together.) Cut each into small pieces and place in the bottom of a serving bowl. Pour the sherry and brandy over them.

2 Heat the milk until it steams. Beat the eggs and sugar together and pour in the hot milk. Mix, return to the pan, and heat gently, stirring, until the custard thickens. Allow to cool slightly, then pour it over the sponge cakes and leave until cold.

3 Spread two-thirds of the cream over the trifle. Decorate the trifle with rosettes made from the remaining cream and angelica leaves, if using. Chill the trifle until ready to eat. Decorate it with edible flowers just before serving, if you like.

a 9-inch sponge cake or 6 split ladyfingers

2–3 tablespoons seedless raspberry jam

4–5 tablespoons sherry

4–5 tablespoons brandy

2½ cups milk

4 eggs

2 tablespoons sugar

2 cups whipping cream, whipped

To Serve:

small piece of angelica, cut into leaves (optional)

edible flowers (optional)

Serves 8–10

Preparation time: 20–25 minutes plus cooling

Cooking time: 5–8 minutes

shortbread

2 sticks (1 cup) butter

½ cup sugar plus extra for sprinkling

½ cup cornstarch

2½ cups all-purpose flour

Makes 32 fingers
Preparation time: 15 minutes
Cooking time: 1½–2 hours

1 Cream the butter and sugar together until light and fluffy. Sift in the cornstarch and flour and mix well to combine. Press into an oblong pan, approximately 12 x 8 inches, and mark with the prongs of a fork.

2 Bake in a preheated oven, 275°F, for 30 minutes, then reduce the oven temperature to 250°F and cook for a further 1–1½ hours.

3 Remove the shortbread from the oven and cut into 32 even-size fingers. Sprinkle with the sugar and leave to cool slightly in the pan, before transferring to a wire rack to cool until firm. Store in an airtight container.

■ This mixture can also be rolled out thinly and cut into circular biscuits. Sometimes a little semolina is added to give a more crunchy texture.

baked scones

1 Sift the flour, cream of tartar, baking soda, and salt into a mixing bowl and rub in the butter with your fingertips until the mixture resembles fine breadcrumbs. Stir in the sugar and add enough milk to mix to a soft dough.

2 Turn the dough onto a floured surface, knead lightly, and roll out to ¾ inch thick. Using a cookie cutter or a glass, cut out 2-inch rounds.

3 Place the rounds on a floured baking sheet and brush with milk. Bake in a preheated oven, 425°F, for 10 minutes. Transfer to a wire rack to cool. Serve with butter or whipped cream and jam.

2 cups all-purpose flour

1 teaspoon cream of tartar

½ teaspoon baking soda

pinch of salt

½ stick (¼ cup) butter

2 tablespoons sugar

½ cup milk plus extra for glazing

To Serve:

butter or whipped cream

jam

Makes about 10
Preparation time: 10 minutes
Cooking time: 10 minutes

pecan pie

1 To make the pastry, sift the flour into a bowl, add the butter, and rub it in with your fingertips until the mixture resembles fine breadcrumbs. Stir in the sugar, then add enough water to make a firm dough. Knead the pastry dough briefly on a lightly floured surface, then roll it out and line an 11 x 7-inch baking sheet with sides. Chill the pastry-lined pan for 30 minutes.

2 To make the filling, mix the sugar, molasses, syrup, butter, and vanilla extract in a bowl. Stir in the lemon zest and beaten eggs and mix well. Chop half the pecans and add to the filling mixture. Pour into the prepared pie crust.

3 Arrange the remaining pecans over the top of the pie. Bake in a preheated oven, 350°F, for 45–50 minutes, until the pie shell is golden brown and the filling has set. Leave to cool, then cut into squares to serve.

Shortcrust Pastry:

2½ cups all-purpose flour

2 sticks (1 cup) chilled butter, diced

4 tablespoons sugar

4–6 tablespoons cold water

Filling:

½ cup brown sugar

¼ cup molasses

¼ cup corn syrup

6 tablespoons butter, melted

1 teaspoon vanilla extract

grated zest of 1 lemon

4 eggs, beaten

1¼ cups pecans

Serves 8–10

Preparation time: 25 minutes plus chilling

Cooking time: 45–50 minutes

■ To make a chocolate and pecan pie, add 2 tablespoons sifted unsweetened cocoa powder to the filling mixture. Sprinkle ⅔ cup of grated chocolate over the cooked baked pie.

1 To make the pastry, sift the flour and salt into a bowl. Rub in the butter with your fingertips until the mixture resembles breadcrumbs. Add the water, slowly, to make a stiff dough. Knead the dough lightly, then put it in a plastic bag and chill for 20–30 minutes.

2 Layer the apples with the sugar and spices in a 1-quart pie dish. Roll out the dough on a lightly floured surface to a circle 2 inches larger than the dish. Cut off a strip all around and use it to cover the dampened rim of the dish; brush with water. Cut the dough into strips and make a lattice covering over the apples, sealing the edges. Trim the edges. Brush with water, sprinkle with the sugar to glaze, and bake in a preheated oven, 400°F, for 30–40 minutes.

3 To make the crème à la vanille, cream the egg yolks with the cornstarch and sugar. Bring the milk to a boil, pour onto the egg mixture and stir. Heat gently, stirring until the mixture coats the back of a spoon. Add the vanilla, then strain. Serve with the pie.

Pastry:

2½ cups all-purpose flour

pinch of salt

1 stick (½ cup) butter, diced

3 tablespoons water

Filling:

1½ lb. tart green apples, peeled, cored, and thinly sliced

½ cup brown sugar

1 teaspoon allspice

4 cloves

water and sugar, to glaze

Crème à la Vanille:

2 egg yolks

1 teaspoon cornstarch

2 tablespoons sugar

1¼ cups milk

½ teaspoon vanilla extract

Serves 4–6

Preparation time: 20 minutes plus chilling

Cooking time: 30–40 minutes

spiced apple pie

banoffi pie

1 To make the crust, melt the butter in a pan and stir in the crushed graham crackers. Press the mixture evenly over the base and sides of an 8-inch round, deep fluted tart or quiche pan. Chill until firm.

2 To make the filling, put the butter and sugar in a pan. Heat gently, stirring, until the butter has melted. Stir in the evaporated milk and bring to a boil. Lower the heat and simmer for about 15 minutes, stirring occasionally, until the mixture becomes a caramel color. Pour into the crust, cool, then chill until set.

3 Slice the bananas and toss them in the lemon juice. Reserve a quarter of the bananas for the decoration and spread the rest over the filling. Beat the cream and spread it gently over the top. Decorate with the reserved bananas and sprinkle with the grated chocolate.

Graham Cracker Crust:

1 stick (½ cup) butter

1½ –1¾ cups crushed graham crackers

Filling:

1½ sticks (¾ cup) butter

½ cup plus 2 tablespoons sugar

2 cups condensed milk

2 bananas

1 tablespoon lemon juice

⅔ cup heavy cream

⅓ cup grated dark chocolate

Serves 6–8

Preparation time: 30 minutes plus chilling

Cooking time: 25 minutes

lemon meringue pie

1 Put the flour in a bowl, add the butter, and rub in with your fingertips until the mixture resembles fine breadcrumbs. Stir in the sugar and ground hazelnuts, then add the egg yolk and enough cold water to mix to a firm dough. Knead the dough briefly on a lightly floured surface, then roll out and use to line an 8-inch fluted tart or quiche pan. Chill for 30 minutes, then fill with crumpled foil and bake in a preheated oven, 400°F, for 15 minutes. Remove the foil and bake the tart shell for a further 5 minutes.

2 To make the filling, mix the cornstarch and sugar in a saucepan. Add the water, lemon zest and juice, and stir until well blended. Bring to a boil, stirring until thickened and smooth. Cool slightly. Beat the egg yolks in a bowl, then beat in 2 tablespoons of the lemon sauce. Return this mixture to the pan and cook gently until the sauce has thickened further. Let the sauce cool slightly, then pour it gently into the pastry shell.

3 To make the meringue, beat the egg whites in a clean bowl until stiff and dry. Beat in 1 tablespoon of the sugar, then fold in the rest. Spread the meringue mixture over the pie to cover the filling. Return to the oven for 10 minutes until the meringue is golden. Serve the pie warm or cold.

2 cups all-purpose flour

1¼ sticks (½ cup plus 2 tablespoons) chilled butter, diced

¼ cup sugar

¾ cup ground hazelnuts

1 egg yolk, beaten

2–3 tablespoons water

Filling:

6 tablespoons cornstarch

a scant ½ cup sugar

1½ cups water

grated zest and juice of 2 lemons

3 egg yolks

Meringue:

3 egg whites

½ cup plus 2 tablespoons sugar

Serves 6
Preparation time: 35 minutes plus chilling
Cooking time: 35 minutes

christmas pudding

1 Sift the flour and spices into a large mixing bowl. Add the breadcrumbs, suet, brown sugar, dried fruit, chopped citron and almonds, and the carrot and apple. Stir well. Add the eggs, grated orange zest and juice, and Guinness. Mix together well. Cover and leave overnight in a cool, dry place.

2 Spoon into a lightly greased 2-quart pudding mold. Cover with buttered foil with a center pleat and steam in a saucepan of boiling water for 4 hours, checking the water level from time to time. Set the pudding, still in its mold, aside until it is completely cold. Remove it from the pudding mold, wrap it in wax paper, and then foil, and store in a cool, dry place for up to 3 months.

3 To serve the pudding, unwrap it and re-steam it in the pudding mold for 1 hour. Tilt it out of the pudding mold and serve. To flame the pudding, warm the brandy or rum in a small saucepan. Pour the alcohol over the pudding and ignite immediately.

■ This pudding is traditionally served at Christmas in Britain. It improves with keeping as it allows the mixture to mature.

1½ cups all-purpose flour

pinch of ground cloves

a slightly larger pinch of ground ginger

1 generous teaspoon grated nutmeg

1 generous teaspoon ground cinnamon

½ cup fresh white breadcrumbs

½ cup chopped suet

½ cup brown sugar

¾ cup golden raisins

¾ cup currants

¾ cup raisins

¾ cup chopped citron

¾ cup chopped almonds

1 cup grated carrot

¾ cup grated apple

2 eggs, beaten

grated zest and juice of 1 small orange

⅔ cup Guinness

3 tablespoons brandy or rum, to flame (optional)

Serves 10–12

Preparation time: 20 minutes plus standing

Cooking time: 4 hours, then 1 hour before serving

bread & butter pudding

1 Use 1 tablespoon of the butter to grease a 5-cup ovenproof serving dish.

2 Butter the bread and spread it with apricot jam. Cut into small triangles. Layer the bread in the dish, sprinkling the citron and golden raisins between the layers. Heat the milk and sugar to just below boiling point. Whisk in the beaten eggs, then strain them over the bread and butter. Leave to soak for 30 minutes.

3 Place the dish in a bain-marie (see below). Bake in a preheated oven, 350°F, for 45 minutes, then increase the heat to 375°F and cook for a further 10–15 minutes, or until crisp and golden on top and just set. Serve at once with cream, if you like.

3 tablespoons butter

4 slices white bread, crusts removed

¼ cup apricot jam

2 tablespoons chopped citron

3 tablespoons golden raisins

2 cups milk

2 tablespoons sugar

2 eggs, beaten

Serves 4

Preparation time: 10 minutes plus soaking

Cooking time: about 1 hour

■ To make a bain-marie, place the dish in a large roasting pan and pour boiling water into the pan to come at least halfway up the sides of the dish.

apricot & almond crumble

1 If using fresh apricots, cut in half and remove the pits and, if you wish, crack a few of the pits and remove the kernels. Place the fresh apricots and kernels, or the cooked dried apricots, in the bottom of a 5-cup buttered pie dish. Sprinkle the granulated sugar and almonds over it, if using.

2 Mix the flour, superfine sugar, and ground almonds together and rub in the butter until the mixture resembles soft breadcrumbs. Spread lightly over the fruit.

3 Bake in a preheated oven, 400°F, for 20 minutes, then reduce the oven temperature to 350°F and cook for a further 20–30 minutes, or until golden brown. Serve the crumble hot, with custard or lightly whipped cream, if you like.

1–1½ lb. fresh apricots or 2 cups dried apricots, soaked overnight

2 tablespoons granulated sugar (optional)

½ cup blanched almonds (optional)

1 cup all-purpose flour

⅓ cup superfine or granulated sugar

1¼ cups ground almonds

1½ sticks (¾ cup) unsalted butter

Serves 4–6

Preparation time: 15–25 minutes plus soaking (if using dried apricots)

Cooking time: 40–50 minutes

bakewell tart

1 Roll out the pastry on a lightly floured clean surface and use it to line an 8-inch fluted tart or quiche pan. Prick the base lightly and spread the jam over it.

2 Beat the eggs and sugar together until they are thick and creamy. Beat in the butter a little at a time, then fold in the ground almonds. Mix well, then pour the mixture into the prepared pastry case.

3 Place on a hot baking sheet and bake in a preheated oven, 400°F, for 25–30 minutes, or until set and golden brown. Serve the tart hot or cold.

½ quantity Shortcrust Pastry (see Pecan Pie, page 84)

2 tablespoons raspberry jam

4 eggs

½ cup superfine or granulated sugar

1 stick (½ cup) unsalted butter, melted and cooled

1¼ cups ground almonds

Serves 5–6
Preparation time: 30 minutes
Cooking time: 25–30 minutes

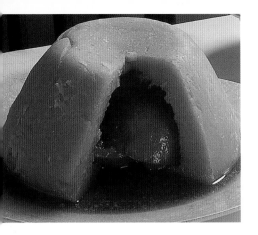

sussex pond pudding

1 Sift the flour into a bowl. Stir in the suet and add the water to make a soft dough. Roll out two-thirds of the dough to line a buttered 1½-quart-deep heatproof bowl.

2 Put half the sugar and dried fruit into the lined bowl. Prick the lemon all over with a skewer and place it upright on top. Cover with the butter in one piece and sprinkle over it the remaining sugar and fruit.

3 Roll out the rest of the pastry to make a lid. Moisten the edges and seal well together. Cover with greased foil, with a pleat in the center, and use a string to tie under the rim of the bowl to secure it. Place in a saucepan filled with enough boiling water to come halfway up the sides of the bowl. Cover and simmer for 2½ hours. Tilt it out onto a hot serving dish. To serve, make sure that everyone gets a bit of the lemon center.

2 cups self-rising flour

⅔ cup chopped suet

⅔ cup water

Filling:

½ cup brown sugar

⅔ cup mixed dried fruit

1 lemon

1 stick (½ cup) unsalted butter

Serves 4–6
Preparation time: 15 minutes plus chilling
Cooking time: 2½ hours

■ The "pond" is the lemon and fruit mixture in the center of the pudding.

treacle pudding

1 Butter a 1-quart-deep heatproof bowl. Then cream the butter and sugar together in a bowl until light and fluffy. Beat in the eggs, one at a time, adding a little of the flour with the second egg. Fold in the remaining flour.

2 Spoon the corn syrup and molasses into the buttered bowl, then put the batter on top. Cover the bowl with buttered foil, making a pleat across the center to allow the pudding to rise. Stand the bowl in a large saucepan with enough boiling water to come about halfway up the sides of the bowl. Boil steadily for 1½–2 hours, adding more boiling water, whenever necessary.

3 To make the sauce, heat the syrup, molasses, and water in a small pan. Tilt out the pudding onto a warmed serving dish and pour the hot sauce over it just before serving.

1 stick (½ cup) butter

½ cup sugar

2 large eggs

1 cup self-rising flour, sifted

3 tablespoons corn syrup

1 tablespoon molasses

Treacle Sauce:

3 tablespoons corn syrup

1 tablespoon molasses

½ tablespoon water

Serves 4
Preparation time: 20–30 minutes
Cooking time: 1½–2 hours

■ To make a steamed jam sponge, use the jam of your choice in place of the corn syrup and molasses in both the bottom of the basin and in the sauce. Apricot and plum jam are particularly good.

index